THE NEGATIVE

Writer **Robbie Thompson**

Artists **Stacey Lee** (#9) &
Tana Ford (#10–13)

Color Artist **Ian Herring**
Letterer **VC's Travis Lanham**
Cover Artist **Helen Chen**

Assistant Editor **Allison Stock**
Associate Editor **Devin Lewis**
Editor **Nick Lowe**

Collection Editor: **Jennifer Grünwald**
Associate Managing Editor: **Kateri Woody**
Associate Editor: **Sarah Brunstad**
Editor, Special Projects: **Mark D. Beazley**
VP Production & Special Projects: **Jeff Youngquist**
SVP Print, Sales & Marketing: **David Gabriel**
Book Designer: **Adam Del Re**

Editor in Chief **Axel Alonso**
Chief Creative Officer: **Joe Quesada**
Publisher: **Dan Buckley**
Executive Producer: **Alan Fine**

SILK VOL. 2: THE NEGATIVE. Contains material originally published in magazine form as SILK #9-13. First printing 2016. ISBN# 978-0-7851-9958-8. Published by MARVEL WORLDWIDE, INC., a subsidiary of MARVEL ENTERTAINMENT, LLC. OFFICE OF PUBLICATION: 135 West 50th Street, New York, NY 10020. **Printed in Canada.** ALAN FINE, President, Marvel Entertainment; DAN BUCKLEY, President, TV, Publishing & Brand Management; JOE QUESADA, Chief Creative Officer; TOM BREVOORT, SVP of Publishing; DAVID BOGART, SVP of Business Affairs & Operations, Publishing & Partnership; C.B. CEBULSKI, VP of Brand Management & Development, Asia; DAVID GABRIEL, SVP of Sales & Marketing, Publishing; JEFF YOUNGQUIST, VP of Production & Special Projects; DAN CARR, Executive Director of Publishing Technology; ALEX MORALES, Director of Publishing Operations; SUSAN CRESPI, Production Manager; STAN LEE, Chairman Emeritus. For information regarding advertising in Marvel Comics or on Marvel.com, please contact Vit DeBellis, Integrated Sales Manager, at vdebellis@marvel.com. For Marvel subscription inquiries, please call 888-511-5480. **Manufactured between 10/28/2016 and 12/5/2016 by SOLISCO PRINTERS, SCOTT, QC, CANADA.**

10 9 8 7 6 5 4 3 2 1

WHEN ATTENDING A SCIENTIFIC DEMONSTRATION, **CINDY MOON** WAS BITTEN BY A RADIOACTIVE SPIDER. AS A RESULT, SHE DEVELOPED ADHESIVE FINGERTIPS AND TOES, THE PROPORTIONAL STRENGTH OF A SPIDER, SUPERHUMAN SPEED AND AGILITY, AND A SPECIAL ORGANIC WEBBING THAT'S WOVEN DIRECTLY OUT OF HER FINGERTIPS. AFTER BEING LOCKED AWAY IN A BUNKER FOR TEN YEARS, CINDY WAS SET FREE AND BECAME THE CRIME-FIGHTING SUPER HERO...

SILK

FOR WEEKS, CINDY MOON, A.K.A. SILK, HAS BEEN WORKING UNDERCOVER FOR **S.H.I.E.L.D.**, HOPING TO TAKE DOWN **BLACK CAT**'S GANG FROM THE INSIDE. RECENTLY, HER STREET CRED GOT A BOOST WHEN AN EVIL VERSION OF HERSELF FROM ANOTHER DIMENSION CAME TO THE MARVEL UNIVERSE AND TOOK HER PLACE FOR A SHORT TIME. WHILE HERE, THE DOPPELGÄNGER WENT ON A CRIME SPREE, AND EVERYONE IS HOLDING SILK RESPONSIBLE FOR IT, FOR BETTER AND WORSE. ON THE ONE HAND, BLACK CAT IS PLEASED THAT SILK HAS STARTED TO TURN TO A MORE CRIMINAL LIFESTYLE; ON THE OTHER, CINDY'S S.H.I.E.L.D. HANDLER, **MOCKINGBIRD**, ISN'T.

HEADQUARTERS OF THE FACT CHANNEL.
SILK CRIME SPREE? SILK CRIME SPREE? SILK CRIME SPREE?
SO, WHAT DO YOU THINK? HAS SILK REALLY GONE BAD?
WHO CARES? WHERE THE HELL IS CINDY?
SHE'S STILL NOT ANSWERING HER CELL?
NO. AND WE NEED TO TALK. I FOUND SOMETHING ABOUT THAT DOCTOR SHE ASKED US TO LOOK FOR.
FACT
CHANNEL
DR. KAPOOR? THE DUDE WHO DISAPPEARED?
I RAN A PROPERTY SEARCH, JUST TO SEE IF HIS NAME APPEARED ON ANY LEASES.
HE POPPED UP ON A LIST OF PEEPS WHO RENTED FROM C & B--CONNOR & BRENNAN PROPERTIES, HOLDING COMPANY FOR A BUNCH OF BUILDINGS IN THE CITY.
ACCORDING TO THIS, C & B WENT BELLY-UP.
YUP-- AND THEIR RECORDS ARE A MESS. KAPOOR'S NAME IS THERE, BUT NO MATCH TO A SPECIFIC ADDY.
SO, I FIGURED WE COULD POUND THE PAVEMENT, GO DOOR-TO-DOOR. OLD-SCHOOL STYLE.
THERE'S A LOT OF GROUND TO COVER. IT WOULD GO FASTER IF THERE WERE THREE OF US.
ALREADY ON IT.
C'MON, CINDY...

"...WHERE THE HELL ARE YOU?"
S.H.I.E.L.D. FIELD OFFICE.
MIDTOWN MANHATTAN.
SORRY TO PULL YOU OUT OF YOUR MEETING, SPIDER-MAN, BUT I NE--
ALL GOOD, THERE'S A CRISIS ACROSS TOWN ANYWAY, SO TIME TO PUT ON THE TIGHTS.
AND, DUDE, WHEN I'M IN A BOARD ROOM. IT'S JUST PETER.
FINE: WHERE THE HELL IS SILK, PETER?
I DON'T KNOW.
BUT...YOU TALKED TO SPIDER-WOMAN. SILK WASN'T RESPONSIBLE FOR THE CRIME SPREE--*
RIGHT. EVIL SILK WAS RESPONSIBLE.
I THINK SHE PREFERS NEFARIOUS SILK.
*AS SEEN IN THE THRILLING SPIDER-WOMEN CROSSOVER EVENT--GO CHECK IT OUT, WE'LL WAIT! ARE YOU BACK? OKAY, LET'S DO THIS...
WHY ISN'T GOOD SILK RETURNING ANY CALLS?
EVIL SILK'S SUCCESS PUT GOOD SILK IN OVER HER HEAD.
WE'LL FIND HER.
"WE"? WHERE ARE YOU?
INDIA. PROBABLY.
IS SHE IN PROBABLY INDIA WITH YOU?
NO. AND MY BET IS...

"...SILK IS AS FAR FROM ME AS POSSIBLE."
PARKER INDUSTRIES, BROOKLYN DIVISION.
YOU SURE YOU KNOW WHERE YOU'RE GOING?
UH, YEAH. OF COURSE I KNOW WHERE I'M GOING.
I HAVE NO IDEA WHERE I'M GOING.
I BROKE IN HERE A WEEK AGO.
I DID NOT BREAK IN HERE A WEEK AGO.
EVIL ME FROM EARTH-65 BROKE IN HERE. AS WELL AS A DOZEN OR MORE HIGH-SECURITY FACILITIES IN NEW YORK.
SHE'S A MASTER THIEF. SO NOW BLACK CAT THINKS I'M A MASTER THIEF.
I AM NOT NOW, NOR WILL I EVER BE, A MASTER THIEF.
I'M NOT A MASTER ANYTHING OUTSIDE OF DISASTER. IS IT TOO LATE TO CHANGE MY NAME TO MASTER DISASTER?
I SHOULD JUST CALL MOCKINGBIRD BACK.
BUT NOOOOO, I JUST HAD TO BE MASTER DISASTER.
HOPE I DIDN'T ALREADY STEAL WHATEVER YOU'RE LOOKING FOR.
UM, WHAT ARE YOU LOOKING FOR?
LITTLE OF THIS. LITTLE OF THAT.

SEE? TOLDJA I KNEW WHERE I WAS GOING.
AND YET YOU DON'T KNOW HOW TO CRACK THIS SAFE YOU BROKE INTO BEFORE.
THAT'S UM, AN UPGRADED SAFE. THEY INSTALLED IT AFTER I DID MY THING.
SO, WHAT DO YOU NEED IN THAT SAFE?
A LIE DETECTOR.
UM, SERIOUSLY?
NAH. IT'S SOME TECH DESIGNED TO SANITIZE A ROOM IN MINUTES.
FOR DO-GOODERS, IT KILLS GERMS.
FOR US, IT'S THE PERFECT WAY TO WIPE A CRIME SCENE.
CLICK
TA-DA. WE WERE NEVER HERE.
UM, CAT--
INTRUDER ALERT!

REALLY? YOU DIDN'T THINK TO MENTION THIS PLACE HAS GIANT SPIDER-BOT SECURITY GUARDS?
UM, THOSE ARE NEW, TOO.
PROBABLY TIME TO GO, RIGHT?
THWIP
THWIP
RELAX, I PUT ALL THE OUTGOING SECURITY FEEDS ON A RUNNING LOOP AS SOON AS WE GOT IN THIS ROOM.
RIGHT. THAT'S... UH...THAT'S WHAT I DID BEFORE. WHEN I DID THIS BEFORE. WHICH I DID. BEFORE.
OH MAN, I'M LITERALLY THE WORST AT THIS.

ARE YOU OKA--
BZZZZT
GAH!
CAT!
I GOT YOU, BOSS.
BBZZZZZZZZTT
INTRUDER ALLLEEEER1111001001--
AND AWAY WE GO--
NO, WAIT, DON'T--

SHOOOK
PERFECT.
WHAT?
WE REALLY NEED TO WORK ON OUR COMMUNICATION SKILLS.
WHAT DO YOU MEAN? WE'RE TALKING.
WE SHOULD HAVE TALKED *BEFORE.*
I SET THE SECURITY FEEDS ON A LOOP.
RIGHT. THAT'S A GOOD THING--
THAT LOOP RESETS EVERY FORTY-FIVE MINUTES THE SECOND THOSE DOORS CLOSE.

VVZZZZZZZ
MEANING...
WE'RE STUCK HERE FOR FORTY-FIVE MINUTES.
STUCK HERE?
IF THAT ELEVATOR DOESN'T SQUASH US.
WE REALLY NEED TO WORK ON OUR COMMUNICATION SKILLS.
VVZZZ
CHOOOM

WE'RE TRAPPED DOWN HERE.
IT'S NOT FOREVER.
IT'S JUST FORTY-FIVE MINUTES.
OKAY.
LET'S BE PRODUCTIVE WITH OUR NEWFOUND TIME AND WORK ON OUR COMMUNICATION SKILLS.
YOU TOLD ME YOU WERE LOCKED AWAY. YOU NEVER TOLD ME WHY. SPILL.
DON'T DO IT, CIN. KEEP HER OUT, CIN.
OR...TELL HER EVERYTHING. WELL, NOT EVERYTHING.
I MASSAGE SOME OF IT-- LEAVING OUT SPIDER-BITES AND SPIDER-BRIDES.
BUT SHE GETS THE GIST.
AND THE CRAZY PART?
SHE GETS ME.
TOOK A LOT OF COURAGE TO MAKE THAT DECISION.
AND A LOT OF STRENGTH TO SURVIVE.

EVERYONE I KNOW, AND IT'S A BAD GUY WHO ACTUALLY GETS ME.
WHY?
OKAY, YOUR TURN.
MY TURN WHAT?
I WAS LOCKED AWAY. AFTER ALL THAT, I CHOSE TO TAKE WHAT'S MINE. WORK FOR YOU. THAT'S WHY I WENT BAD--
"MY POWER HAS ALWAYS BEEN LUCK.
"BUT FOR SOMEONE AS LUCKY AS ME, I JUST COULDN'T CATCH BREAK.
"DIDN'T MATTER IF I WAS A CROOK...
"...OR A HERO.
"BOTH GAVE ME NOTHING BUT PROBLEMS.
"I WAS... TIRED.
"ALL MY PLANS WENT OUT THE WINDOW.
"MY NEST EGG? GONE.

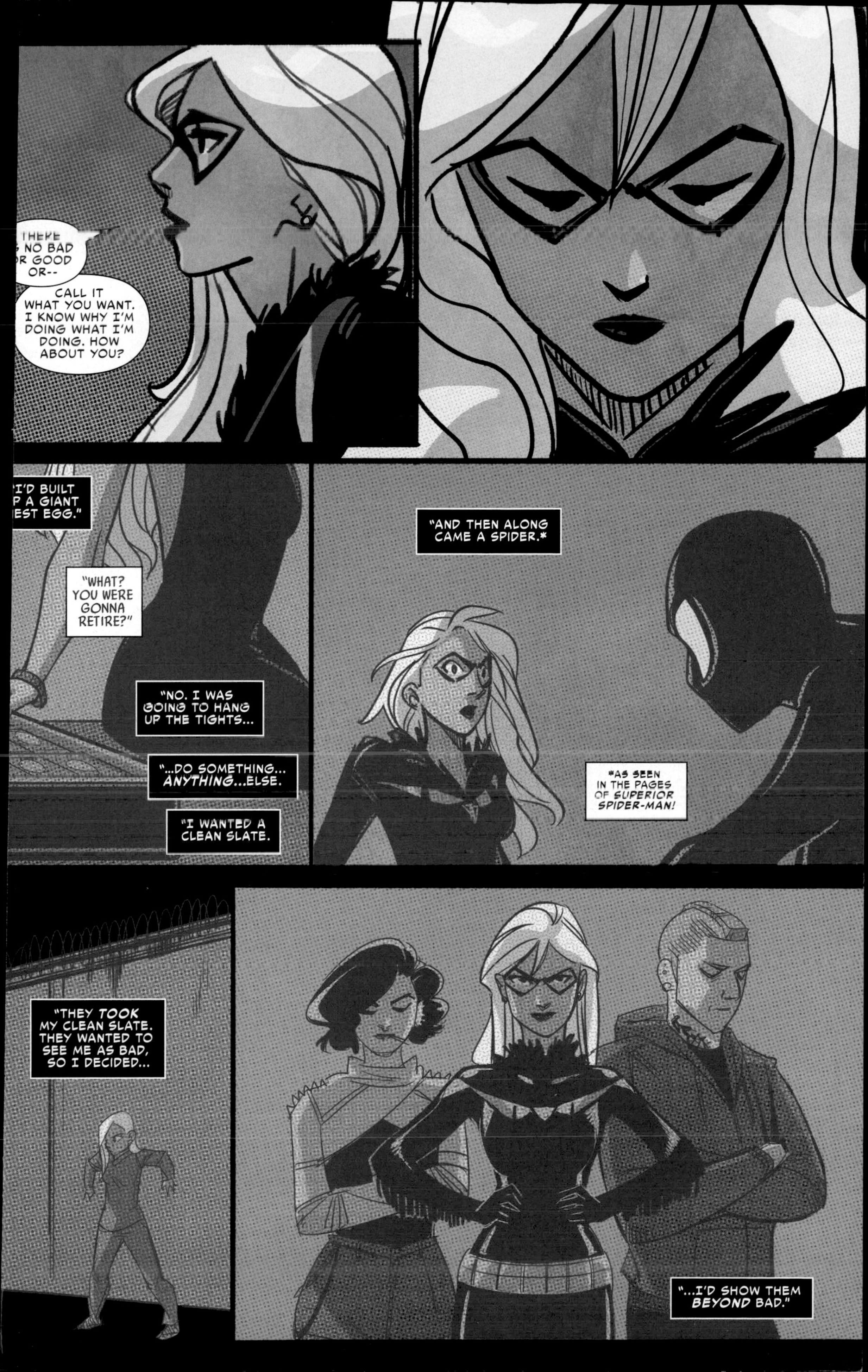
THERE S NO BAD OR GOOD OR--
CALL IT WHAT YOU WANT. I KNOW WHY I'M DOING WHAT I'M DOING. HOW ABOUT YOU?
I'D BUILT P A GIANT EST EGG."
"WHAT? YOU WERE GONNA RETIRE?"
"NO. I WAS GOING TO HANG UP THE TIGHTS...
"...DO SOMETHING... *ANYTHING*...ELSE.
"I WANTED A CLEAN SLATE.
"AND THEN ALONG CAME A SPIDER.*
*AS SEEN IN THE PAGES OF *SUPERIOR SPIDER-MAN!*
"THEY *TOOK* MY CLEAN SLATE. THEY WANTED TO SEE ME AS BAD, SO I DECIDED...
"...I'D SHOW THEM *BEYOND* BAD."

SHOW "THEM"? THEM WHO? SPIDER--
EVERYONE.
CAN I ASK YOU SOMETHING?
SHOOT.
YOUR PLAN TO HANG UP THE TIGHTS...
...DO YOU THINK IT WOULD HAVE WORKED?
VVZZZZZZZ
TIME'S UP. LET'S GO.

I'M GONNA STRETCH MY LEGS. TAKE THIS BACK TO MY OFFICE.
YOU SURE?
OF COURSE.
I TRUST YOU, SILK.
SHE TRUSTS ME.
BLACK CAT TRUSTS ME.
AND I FEEL HORRIBLY GUILTY ABOUT BETRAYING HER TRUST. WHY?

I MEAN, WHY WOULD I FEEL GUILTY FOR BETRAYING THE TRUST OF A KNOWN CRIMINAL?
HOW MANY PEOPLE HAVE YOU TRUSTED IN YOUR LIFE? REALLY TRUSTED.
I TRUST YOU.
PSYCHIAT
PSYCHIAT
PSYCHIAT
2014
2015
2016
HOW MANY PEOPLE OUTSIDE THIS ROOM?
MY FAMILY.
MY EX, HECTOR.
SO...FOUR PEOPLE. FOUR PEOPLE WHO AREN'T EXACTLY IN MY LIFE RIGHT NOW.
HAVE YOU SEEN HECTOR SINCE YOU GOT OUT?
PERHAPS YOU SHOULD TALK TO HIM, YOU HAVE HISTORY, HE MIGHT--
I RAN INTO HIM ONCE. HE'S ENGAGED.
I SEE. AND HOW DOES THAT MAKE YOU FEEL?
SAD. AND THEN GUILTY FOR BEING SAD. I MEAN...HE DESERVES TO BE HAPPY.
SO DO YOU, CINDY.

ANYTHING?
NOPE.
HOW MANY MORE ADDRESSES ARE LEFT?
A ZILLION.
C & B HAS THE WEIRDEST PROPERTIES-- BASEMENTS AND ROOFTOP PENTHOUSES...WHO THE HELL WERE THESE PEOPLE?
SOMETHING IS WEIRD ABOUT THIS. I MEAN, WE DUG THROUGH EVERYTHING AND NOTHING CAME UP FOR THIS DUDE KAPOOR.
NOW SUDDENLY THIS WEIRDNESS POPS UP?
LOOK, MAYBE THESE ARE ALL DEAD ENDS.
BUT THERE'S SMOKE HERE.
AND WE OWE IT TO CINDY TO FIND OUT IF THERE'S ANY FIRE.
RIGHT. CINDY DOESN'T-RETURN-TEXTS-AND-PHONE-CALLS MOON. WE OWE IT TO HER?
C'MON, WE'LL GET SNACKS.
DON'T PLY ME WITH SNACKS.
I BET ONE OF THESE PLACES PROBABLY HAS A NICE VIEW. WE'LL HAVE A PICNIC.
SIGH I AM A SUCKER FOR A PICNIC.

PEOPLE CAN BE FRIENDS WITH THEIR EXES.
I'M FRIENDS WITH PETER.
WAIT, ARE WE FRIENDS? DO I ACTUALLY HAVE ANY FRIENDS?
WHAT ARE YOU DOING, CIN?
CERVANTES, H
PHAM, M
BZZZZT
YEAH?
HI...UH, HECTOR, IT'S--
NO, HE DOESN'T LIVE HERE ANYMORE. HASN'T FOR MONTHS. THE SUPER STILL HASN'T CHANGED THE BUZZER.
OH, I'M SORRY, DO YOU HAPPEN TO HAVE ANY CONTACT--
NOPE. SORRY.
I DESERVE TO BE HAPPY, HUH?

I WAS HAPPY HERE. FOR A TIME.
IN THE BUNKER.
MY BUNKER.
YOU'RE TERRIBLE AT RETURNING PHONE CALLS.
I'M SORRY.
WE NEED TO TALK.
CAN WE CHAT OUTSIDE?
WHO'S WITH YOU?
SORRY. DIDN'T MEAN TO SNEAK UP ON YOU.
I'M NOT USED TO TALKING TO PEOPLE OTHER THAN ME IN HERE.
IT'S JUST ME. AND I JUST WANT TO TALK.

ABOUT LAST NIGHT. I WAS HOPING IF I DID ONE MORE JOB... I'D FINALLY FIGURE OUT WHAT SHE'S UP TO...I WAS WRONG.
I'LL HAVE MY TEAM DISABLE IT. YOU TAKE IT BACK TO CAT AND THEN... YOU'RE DONE.
BLACK CAT ISN'T--
BLACK CAT IS A CRIMINAL. ALWAYS HAS BEEN--
THAT'S NOT--
--ALWAYS WILL BE.
YOU WORKING UNDERCOVER?
IT'S OVER.
I KNOW.
BLACK CAT'S GOTTA GO DOWN.
I KNOW.
IT'S TIME FOR SILK TO BE A GOOD GUY AGAIN.

ABOUT LAST NIGHT. I WAS HOPING IF I DID ONE MORE JOB... I'D FINALLY FIGURE OUT WHAT SHE'S UP TO...I WAS WRONG.
I'LL HAVE MY TEAM DISABLE IT. YOU TAKE IT BACK TO CAT AND THEN... YOU'RE DONE.
BLACK CAT ISN'T--
BLACK CAT IS A CRIMINAL. ALWAYS HAS BEEN--
THAT'S NOT--
--ALWAYS WILL BE.
YOU WORKING UNDERCOVER?
IT'S OVER.
I KNOW.
BLACK CAT'S GOTTA GO DOWN.

I KNOW.
ALL RIGHT, WHAT EXACTLY ARE WE STEALING?
A LIE DETECTOR.
I TRUST YOU, SILK.
IT'S TIME FOR SILK TO BE A GOOD GUY AGAIN.

SO, IT'S COME TO THIS.
MY LIFE IS AN ACTUAL DUMPSTER FIRE.
I'D MOVE, BUT I'M NINETY PERCENT CERTAIN SOMETHING IS INTERNALLY BLEEDING-SLASH-BROKEN.
THIS IS ALL TOTALLY MY FAULT.
TOTALLY AVOIDABLE.
OH, CINDY...
ALL THINGS END

...WHY DO YOU NEVER *LISTEN?*
HEY, CINDY!
CIN...?
CIN!
SILK
SILK
SILK
CIN, WE REALLY NEED TO TALK--
IT'S ABOUT--
GUYS, I'M SORRY, I GOTTA-- I CAN'T--
LATER, OKAY?
...AND THE FACT THAT YOU'RE A SUPER HERO.
--YOUR FAMILY.
SUPER *VILLAIN*, YOU MEAN.
YOU DON'T MEAN THAT, LOLA.
NO. *SIGH* WHAT ARE WE SUPPOSED TO DO NOW?

Don't go back to the Cat.
BZZ BZZZ
Thirty minutes. Stark bldg. Greenpoint.
"...I GET KNOCKED DOWN, BUT I GET UP AGAIN..."
HEY.
"HEY"? "HEY"? THAT'S ALL YOU'VE GOT FOR ME?
WHAT'S WRONG WITH HEY?
ARE YOU SURE YOU'RE READY FOR THIS? SAY THE WORD, SILK...

...SAY THE WORD AND WE WALK. YOUR S.H.I.E.L.D. DAYS CAN BE DONE. LIKE I'VE BEEN SAYING WE SHOULD ALL ALONG.
NO. I GOT THIS. BLACK CAT IS BREAKING INTO THE STARK BUILDING IN GREENPOINT. THIRTY MINUTES.
WE'RE ON OUR WAY. YOU WON'T BE ALONE, SILK. I PROMISE.
"BLACK CAT IS BREAKING INTO THE STARK BUILDING IN GREENPOINT. THIRTY MINUTES."
"WE'RE ON OUR WAY."
"YOU WON'T BE ALONE, SILK. I PROMISE."

CLICK
END CALL
CINDY...
WHOA. IT'S YOU AGAIN.
OKAY, YOU NEED TO START TALKING, STRANGER. WHO ARE YOU?
A FRIEND.
I DON'T HAVE ANY FRIENDS.
SERIOUSLY. WHO ARE YOU?

OKAY, GOOD TALK.
I GOT PLACES TO BE AND YOU GOT THINGS NOT TO SAY.
I DON'T KNOW WHO YOU ARE, BUT DO ME A SOLID...
...STAY AWAY FROM ME.
IN FAIRNESS, HE WASN'T SAYING MUCH...
...BUT I STILL SHOULD HAVE LISTENED...

ALL RIGHT, ALL DIVISIONS MOVE IN. PACKAGE IS IN THE BUILDING.
REPEAT, PACKAGE IS IN THE BUILDING.

STARTING TO THINK YOU WEREN'T GOING TO MAKE IT.
I'M FASHIONABLY LATE.
HOW DID YOU TURN THE POWER OFF TO THE WHOLE BUILDING?
YOU KNOW ME. I'M JUST LUCKY THAT WAY.
SO. WHAT ARE WE STEALING?
THIS BELT.
DOESN'T REALLY GO WITH MY MASK, DOES IT?
I THINK YOU CAN MAKE IT WORK. MIGHT BE NICE TO ADD A SPLASH OF COLOR TO YOUR WARDROBE.
SO... WHAT IS IT?
IT'S A PROTOTYPE...
...FOR A *TELEPORTER*.
PACKAGE IS OUT OF POCKET, REPEAT--
WHAT--
THERE'S NO TIME. *MOVE. NOW.*

HUH. WELL. IT WORKS. SO, WE'RE DONE?
WE ARE MOST DEFINITELY DONE.

DON'T WORRY. THEY'RE JUST HERE TO WATCH.
TO SEE WHAT I DO WITH PEOPLE WHO...
...DOUBLE...
...CROSS...
...ME!

I'M SORRY.
TRULY.
WHAT DID THEY OFFER YOU? MONEY?
THEY OFFERED TO HELP FIND MY FAMILY.
AND HOW'D THAT WORK OUT FOR YOU?
DON'T DO THIS.
KINDA FORCING MY HAND HERE, SUNSHINE.
AAGH!

WE DON'T HAVE TO FIGHT AT ALL.
TURN YOURSELF IN. TELL THEM WHAT YOU TOLD ME.
AND GO TO JAIL FOR THE NEXT SIXTY YEARS?
PASS.
YOU'RE NOT BAD. NOT ALL BAD.
NOT YET, ANYWAY.
YOU'RE WRONG, SILK.
I'M ALL BAD.
AND YOU...
...ARE NOTHING.
AAAAAGH!!!
GAAAGH!
8

SEE? I SHOULD HAVE JUST LISTENED.
BUT I NEVER DO THAT.
AND NOW I MAY NEVER GET TO LEARN HOW.
I GOT ONE CHANCE HERE. STORE UP WHAT LITTLE STRENGTH I HAVE...
...TAKE THE BEATING, WAIT FOR THE PERFECT SHOT.
BEND MY KNEES, AND...
...HELP BLACK CAT FOLLOW THROUGH.
KRACK
SMASSSH
BLACK CAT--
SHUT UP.
NOBODY MOVE.
CLICK

AND IT WORKED. I ESCAPED!
FOR THIRTY SECONDS.
IT'S OVER.

I WIN.
NO...

...YOU LOSE.

THIS WAS ALL ABOUT BUYING TIME.
MOST OF S.H.I.E.L.D. JUST FINISHED RAIDING YOUR HIDEOUT.
AND THE REST OF THEIR AGENTS?
THEY'RE MAKING FRIENDS WITH YOUR CREW.
HANDS IN THE AIR, NOW!
TURN YOURSELF IN. I'LL TESTIFY ON YOUR BEHA--

DIE, PIG!
I'M SORRY.
TELL SOMEONE WHO CARES.
...YOU'RE... WRONG... YOU'RE NOT BAD...
...NOT ALL BAD...

DAMN YOU...
BOSS... WE GOTTA GO. THIS PLACE IS CRAWLING WITH S.H.I.E.L.D.
BOSS, DO YOU HEAR ME? IT WAS A TRAP. THEY TOOK EVERYTHING. *EVERYTHING.*
NO. NOT *EVERYTHING.*
CLICK

...NONE OF THIS WOULD HAVE BEEN POSSIBLE WITHOUT THE AID OF SILK, WHO WORKED SELFLESSLY UNDERCOVER FOR MONTHS--
FACT CHANNEL
LIVE
MOCKINGBIRD
AGENT OF S.H.I.E.L.D.
PRESS
BREAKING NEWS
MASSIVE FIRE DOWNTOWN • S.H.I.E.L.D. AGENTS ON THE SCENE • INJURIES LI
SEE? I TOLD YOU.
I TOLD YOU SILK WAS A GOOD GUY. GIRL.
WHATEVER.
NEW STORY! MEDIA: WRONG AS ALWAYS!
THANKS SO MUCH--THAT WAS PERFECT.
ANY TIME.
STILL NO SIGN OF SILK?
NO, MA'AM.
YOU'VE SCANNED EVERYTHING?

"WE CHECKED THE RUBBLE IN THE WAREHOUSE.
"AND THE DEBRIS THAT FELL OFF THE SIDE OF THE BUILDING.
"NO SIGN OF HER.
"SILK'S GONE."

...WHEREAMI...
...AM I DEAD...?
NO. BUT... I AM.
OKAY, THAT'S NOT CREEPY.
LOOK, THANKS FOR THE HELP, BUT SERIOUSLY... WHO ARE YOU?
I TOLD YOU. I'M A FRIEND.
OH MY GOD...
AN OLD FRIEND.
HECTOR?!

DOORWAYS

"WE NEED TO FOCUS ON YOUR ANGER ISSUES, CINDY. WHERE DO YOU THINK THE ANGER COMES FROM?"
"I DON'T KNOW
"IT'S COMFORTING, THOUGH. I'M NEVER ALONE, 'CAUSE IT'S ALWAYS THERE...
" ALWAYS "
"LET'S KEEP IT SIMPLE, THEN.
"WHAT IS MAKING YOU ANGRY RIGHT NOW?"
"RIGHT NOW? MY BOYFRIEND--
"MY EX-BOYFRIEND.
"MY DEAD, EX-BOYFRIEND."
"I'M SORRY, WHAT?"
"IT'S... COMPLICATED."

BEFORE... UNDER NYC...
I DON'T KNOW WHO YOU ARE, OR WHAT THIS IS--
STAND STILL SO I CAN PUNCH YOU PROPERLY.
CINDY, IT'S ME. IT'S HECTOR.
YOU HAVE A CRAZY MEMORY, BUT MINE'S NOT SO BAD EITHER.
YOUR FAVORITE HOCKEY PLAYER IS STEVE YZERMAN, YOU LOVE POKÉMON, BUT ONLY THE ORIGINAL DECK...
...AND YOU TOLD ME YOU LOVED ME FOR THE FIRST TIME AT THE BRONX ZOO.
HECTOR...?
WAIT, CIN--
WHA--?!

I DON'T-- WHY CAN'T I HUG YOU?!
I'M SORRY. I CAN'T KEEP MY FORM UNLESS I'M IN COMBAT.
WHY?
THERE'S NO EASY WAY TO SAY THIS...
CINDY... I'M DEAD.
TELL ME EVERYTHING.
"HE TOLD ME. EVERYTHING.
"STARTING WITH HOW HE BROKE UP WITH HIS FIANCÉE...

"...OR RATHER, HOW SHE BROKE UP WITH HIM.
"HE DIDN'T SAY WHY, AND IS IT LAME THAT I DIDN'T ASK? DON'T ANSWER THAT, I KNOW IT WAS LAME.
"HE GOT A NEW PLACE, ALL ON HIS OWN.
"AND ON HIS FIRST NIGHT THERE...
4B
DISHES
"...SOME LUNATIC IN THE NEXT-DOOR APARTMENT SUMMONED A MONSTER OR A DEMON.
"WHATEVER IT WAS, IT EXPLODED.
"KILLING HECTOR.
"MOSTLY."

I DON'T KNOW WHAT FLOWED THROUGH ME THAT NIGHT. IT WASN'T LIVING OR DEAD.
NOW NEITHER AM I.
I CAN WALK THROUGH WALLS, CARRY A CURRENT, AND SOMETIMES I CAN SEE THE FUTURE.
SERIOUSLY?
I'M KIDDING ABOUT THE FUTURE PART.
NEVER COULD LIE TO YOU.
IT'S TAKEN ME A WHILE TO FIGURE OUT HOW MY BODY WORKS NOW, FROM WALKING TO FLYING-- FROM WHISPERING TO TALKING.
THAT'S WHY YOU HAVEN'T BEEN TOO CHATTY, HUH?
HECTOR... I'M SORRY.
ME, TOO.

HOW DID YOU KNOW I WAS SILK?
YOU NEVER FORGET YOUR FIRST LOVE, CIN.
SOON AS I SAW SILK ON THE NEWS, I JUST KNEW.
SO, YOU'RE, LIKE, MY GUARDIAN ANGEL?
I GUESS. JUST DON'T CALL ME CLARENCE.
DEAL.
CAN I ASK YOU SOMETHING STRANGE, NOT-CLARENCE?
SURE.
YOUR POWERS... THEY ACTIVATE WHEN YOU'RE IN COMBAT, RIGHT?
RIGHT.
CAN YOU TACKLE ME?
WHAT? WHY WOULD I--

SO, YEAH. I'M ANGRY AT MY EX-BOYFRIEND.
WHY?
HE'S SINGLE AGAIN.
BUT DEAD.

FAIR POINT.
WHAT ELSE?
WELL, THERE'S THE FACT I CAN'T HOLD HIM UNLESS--
WHAT ELSE ARE YOU ANGRY ABOUT, CINDY?
THERE'S NOTHI--
WHAT *ELSE*, CINDY?
BESIDES YOU?
BESIDES ME.
"I'M ANGRY AT MY HANDLER.
"MY *EX*-HANDLER.
"MOCKINGBIRD WAS MY S.H.I.E.L.D. LIAISON WHEN I WAS UNDERCOVER WITH BLACK CAT."

LOOK, BOO, I CAN EXPLAIN, I JUST--

YOU'RE ALIVE.
UM, YEAH. YAY, ME.
BUT BLACK CAT GOT AWAY.
YOU SET HER BACK. YOU DID GOOD, KID.
TRUTH IS, YOU HELD UP YOUR END, AND WE DIDN'T. I'M ASSIGNING MORE AGENTS TO YOUR PARENTS' CASE.
AND I WAS THINKING... MAYBE YOU COULD BE ONE OF THEM.
BUT I SUCK AT BEING A DOUBLE AGENT.
THAT'S BECAUSE YOU SKIPPED THE PART ABOUT BECOMING AN ACTUAL AGENT.
I...I ALREADY HAVE A JOB.
THAT PAYS SQUAT. BESIDES, S.H.I.E.L.D. HAS GREAT DENTAL.
JUST THINK ABOUT IT. OKAY?
"I'M ANGRY AT MY NEW BOSS."

YOU'RE ANGRY SHE OFFERED YOU A JOB?
A JOB WAY ABOVE MY SKILL LEVEL. AND I LIKE THE JOB I HAVE.
OKAY... WHAT ELSE ARE YOU ANGRY ABOUT?
tic
tick
tic
tack
tack
tick
tick
tok
tick

"ANALOG!"

ANALOG, GET IN MY OFFICE, NOW!

"I'M ANGRY AT MY BOSS. MY REAL BOSS."
"WHY?"

"OKAY, THAT'S A LIE. HE'S THE ONLY PERSON I'M NOT ANGRY WITH. LIKE I SAID, I LIKE THE JOB I HAVE. ESPECIALLY NOW."
WAIT, WHAT? BUT YOU'RE NOT MY--
I AM NOW, AND I JUST GAVE YOU A RAISE. NOW GET OUTTA MY OFFICE AND EARN THAT MONEY.
ETHICS IN JOURNALISM
HEY, CIN.
EVERYTHING GO OKAY IN THERE?
I THINK SO. HE JUST YELLED A RAISE AT ME.
NICE.
did i get a Raise?
WHY DON'T YOU COME OVER TONIGHT? WE'VE BEEN TRACKING DOWN--
MATT & ARIANNA 2:30P 6/25
SORRY, GUYS. I GOTTA RUN.
RIGHT. OF COURSE YOU DO.
"AND THAT CONCLUDES MY ANGRY RECAP...CAN I STOP BEING ANGRY NOW?"
EXIT

CINDY...
YES...?
LET ME ASK ANOTHER WAY.
YOU SAID YOU'RE NEVER ALONE BECAUSE YOUR ANGER IS ALWAYS WITH YOU.
DOES THAT SOUND HEALTHY TO YOU?
WHAT DID YOU FEEL *BEFORE* THE ANGER KEPT YOU COMPANY?
WHEN THE DOOR CLOSED, LOCKING YOU IN, WHAT DID YOU FEEL? DON'T THINK, JUST--
AFRAID.
YOUR ANGER KEPT YOU COMPANY WHEN YOU WERE ALONE.
BUT YOU'RE NOT ALONE ANYMORE, CINDY.

"...YOU'RE NOT ALONE ANYMORE."
I FINALLY CAUGHT ONE.
C'MON, ALBERT. YOUR REFLEXES ARE GETTING BETTER.
MAYBE. BUT MY STAMINA? NOT SO MUCH. LET'S EAT ALREADY.
CAN I ASK YOU SOMETHING?
ANYTHING.
WHEN I WAS YOUNGER...DO YOU REMEMBER ME BEING ANGRY?
I MEAN, YOU AND MOM FOUGHT SOMETIMES.
BUT I WOULDN'T DESCRIBE YOU THAT WAY.
WHY?
MY...MY SHRINK THINKS I HAVE ANGER ISSUES.
UNDERSTANDABLE.
IT IS?
CINDY, YOU WERE LOCKED IN A BUNKER FOR A DECADE. I WOULD HAVE LOST WHAT LITTLE OF MY MIND I HAVE LEFT.
YOU WANT TO BE ANGRY, BE ANGRY.
JUST DON'T DO IT ALONE.

"YOU'RE NOT ALONE ANYMORE, CINDY."
Cin, it's Raff-- lunch today?
"THE DOOR THAT WAS LOCKED? THE DOOR THAT KEPT YOU AWAY FROM THE WORLD? THAT DOOR IS OPEN NOW. MANY DOORS ARE OPEN NOW."
"IT'S UP TO YOU TO FIGURE OUT WHICH DOORS TO WALK THROUGH...
"...AND WHICH DOORS TO CLOSE."
CIN?
CIN, WAIT--!

THAT NEWS REPORT WAS FROM YESTERDAY, GENIUS.
WE NEED TO TALK, CIN.
UM, THIS IS, UH...
I'M A COSPLAYER?
YOU JUST SHOT WEBS OUT OF YOUR FINGERTIPS, BRO.
AND THAT...
...IS AWESOME!
WAIT, YOU GUYS AREN'T--
CINDY, THIS IS SO AMAZING, AND YOUR SECRET IS SAFE, AND WE THOUGHT YOU WERE BAD BUT--
I...
I AM NOT ALONE.
I AM NOT ALONE.

I TELL THEM EVERYTHING.
THEY'RE SURPRISED. SAD. ANGRY.
I AM NOT ALONE.
AND THEY TELL ME EVERYTHING.
EVERYTHING THEY'VE LEARNED.
EVERYTHING THEY'VE FOUND.
KAPOOR
DR. KAPOOR HAS A LAB. IT'S BEEN ABANDONED FOR MONTHS. BUT SOMEONE IS STILL PAYING THE RENT.
DID YOU GO THERE?
IT'S KINDA LOCKED. WE NEEDED BACK-UP.
DO YOU GUYS GET MOTION SICKNESS?
NO. WHY?

THIS IS SO--
HEAVY!
CAN WE DO THAT AGAIN?
YEAH, NO.
MAYBE ONE AT A TIME, PIGGYBACK-STYLE?
EYES ON THE PRIZE, GANG.
LOCK PICKS. LITTLE TRICK I LEARNED FROM MY OLD BOSS.
BLACK CAT. IS SHE AS HOT AS SHE LOOKS IN REAL LIFE, OR--
DUDE.
WHAT? YOU WERE THINKING THE SAME--
SILK'S FRIENDS... THEY'RE CIVILIANS.
IF THEY DIE, THEY DIE. ALL THAT MATTERS IS SILK.

camera 1
camera 4
security feed
camera 3
ARE YOU SURE SILK WILL TAKE THE BAIT?
I'M POSITIVE.

TOP-SECRET MAD SCIENTIST LAB. TOP-SECRET MAD SCIENTIST LAB. TOP-SECRET MAD SCIENTIST LAB. TOP-SECRET MAD SCIENTIST LAB.
DUDE.
SORRY, THIS IS MY FIRST ADVENTURE.
IT'S AN *ACTIVITY LOG.*
"GATEWAY ESTABLISHED. FIRST EXPEDITION TOMORROW. KAPOOR, MOON AND MOON."
MY PARENTS... THEY WERE *HERE.*
PLEASE TELL ME I'M NOT THE ONLY ONE THAT JUST PEED THEIR PANTS A LITTLE.
WHERE... WHERE DOES THAT DOOR LEAD?

LET'S FIND OUT.

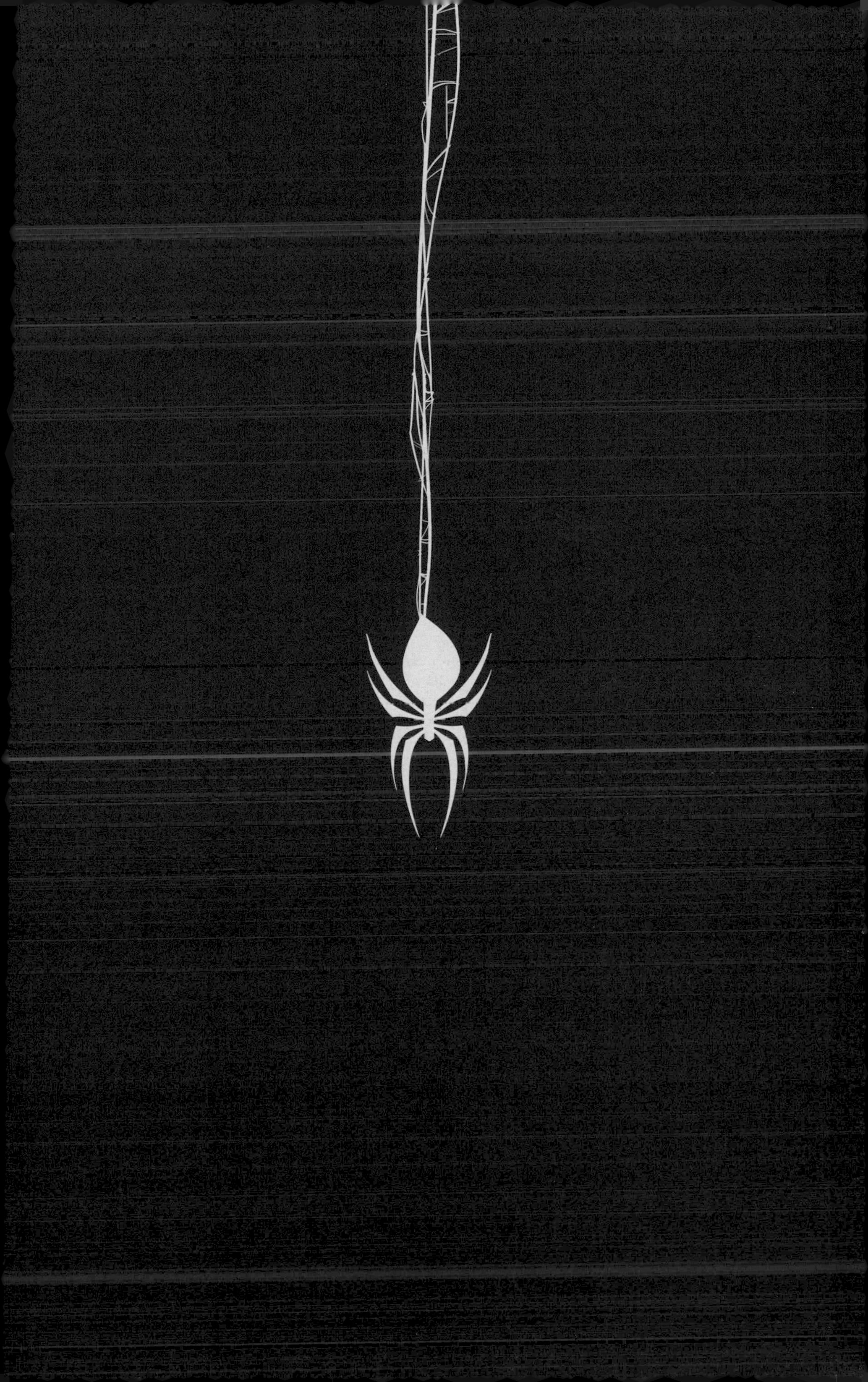

I PACKED YOUR HOCKEY GEAR.
BUT--
YOU CAN WORK ON YOUR BACKHAND.
THANKS, DAD.
CINDY.
I'M GOING TO FIND OUT HOW TO FIX THIS.
AND I'M NOT GIVING UP UNTIL I DO.
EVER.
JUST... JUST KNOW THAT. OKAY?
AND WE'LL ALWAYS BE WITH YOU...

"...ALWAYS."
UM, I'M NOT TRYING TO FREAK OUT, BUT--
WHERE THE HELL ARE WE?!
DEEP BREATH, RAFFERTY. DEEP BREATH.
WE'RE IN THE NEGATIVE ZONE. AND WE'RE OKAY. WE'RE OKAY.
ARE WE OKAY, CIN?
HONESTLY?

I HAVE
YOU GUYS SHOULD HEAD BACK TO THE DOOR.
I CAN--
NO WAY, CIN.
WE GOT YOUR BACK.
AND WE'RE NOT LEAVING THIS PLACE UNTIL WE FIND OUT WHERE YOUR PARENTS ARE.

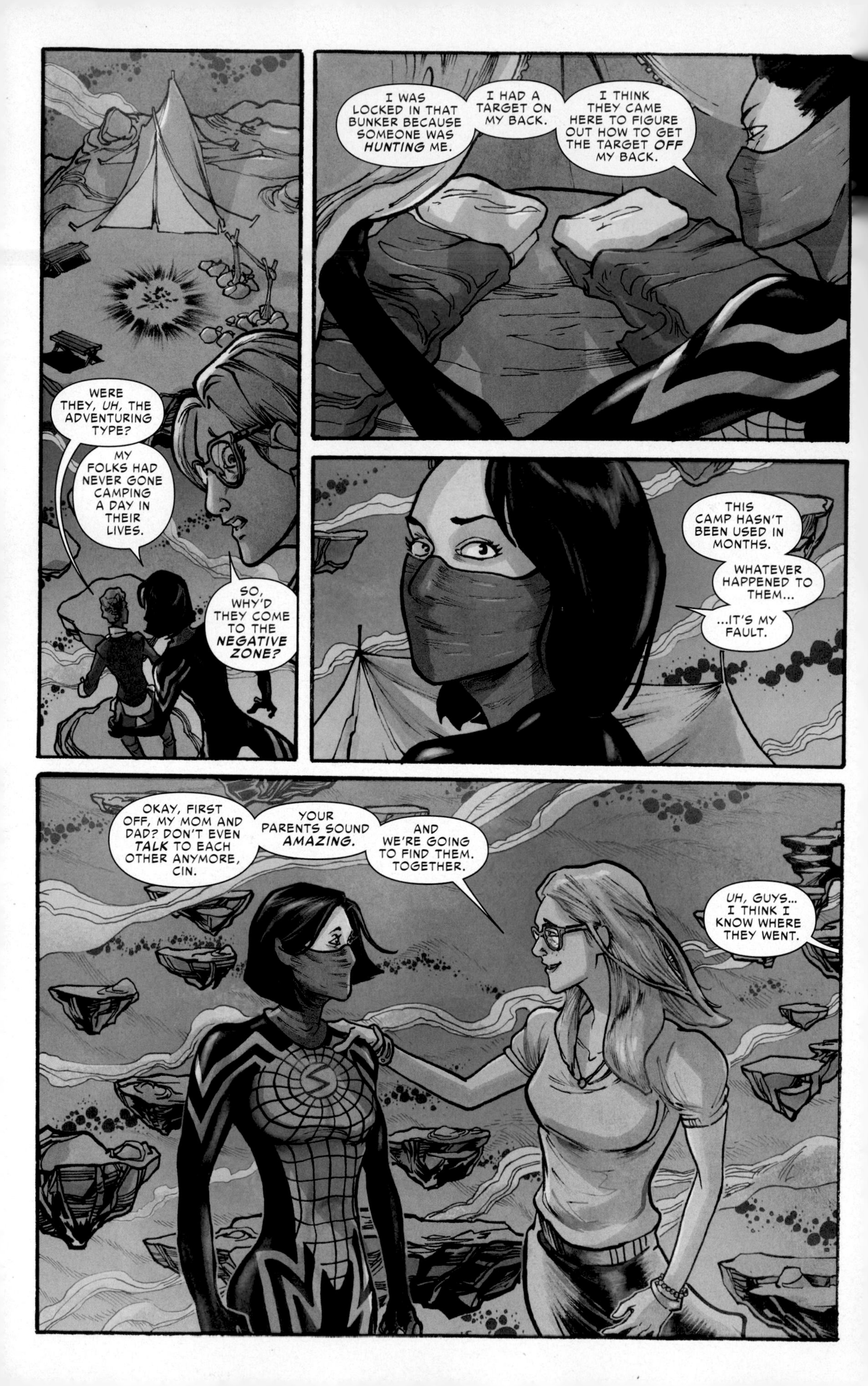
WERE THEY, UH, THE ADVENTURING TYPE?
MY FOLKS HAD NEVER GONE CAMPING A DAY IN THEIR LIVES.
SO, WHY'D THEY COME TO THE NEGATIVE ZONE?
I WAS LOCKED IN THAT BUNKER BECAUSE SOMEONE WAS HUNTING ME.
I HAD A TARGET ON MY BACK.
I THINK THEY CAME HERE TO FIGURE OUT HOW TO GET THE TARGET OFF MY BACK.
THIS CAMP HASN'T BEEN USED IN MONTHS.
WHATEVER HAPPENED TO THEM...
...IT'S MY FAULT.
OKAY, FIRST OFF, MY MOM AND DAD? DON'T EVEN TALK TO EACH OTHER ANYMORE, CIN.
YOUR PARENTS SOUND AMAZING.
AND WE'RE GOING TO FIND THEM. TOGETHER.
UH, GUYS... I THINK I KNOW WHERE THEY WENT.

UM, THIS IS A PARACHUTE...
I THINK THEY JUMPED.
UM, WHAT ARE YOU DOING?
WEAVING.
THWIP
WEAVING WHAT--OH. WAIT. YEAH.
YEAH!
THIS IS GONNA--
SUCK!

WOO-HOO!

OKAY, GUYS, I HAVE NO IDEA WHAT'S BELOW.

SO, ONCE WE LAND, STICK CLOSE TO ME.
HEY, RAFFERTY?
YEAH?

IF WE SURVIVE THIS, LET'S GET A CAT.
IF WE SURVIVE THIS, LET'S GET MARRIED.
THAT WORKS, TOO.

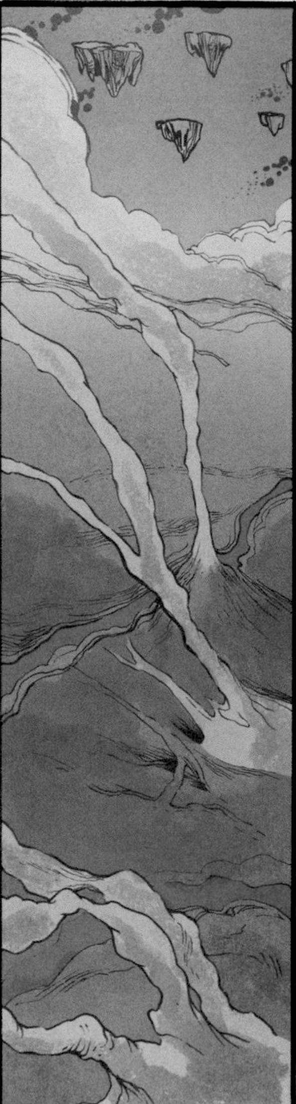

CRAP, TREES!
LOOK OUT--

THWIP
ARE WE ALIVE?
I THINK SO.
WHERE ARE WE NOW, LOLA?
WHAT... WHAT IS *THAT...?*

LOOK LIKE EGGS TO ME?
OKAY, BUT WHAT COULD HAVE LAID AN EGG *THIS* SIZE?
LET'S NOT FIND OUT, 'KAY?
GUYS!
GUYS--ANOTHER PARACHUTE. BUT THIS ONE WAS USED. CINDY, I THINK YOUR PARENTS WERE HERE.
WE'RE CLOSE.
WE'RE IN A DEAD FOREST AND WE JUST FOUND A NEST OF GIANT EGGS.
IS THIS A TYPICAL DAY FOR A SUPER HERO?
KINDA, YEAH.
OH, HEY... I THINK I KNOW WHERE WE ARE...

...WELCOME TO JURASSIC PARK!

ROAR!
ROAR!

IS IT JUST ME, OR IS THAT VILLAGE UNDER ATTACK?
FOLLOW UP: IF IT IS, WHY ARE WE MOVING TOWARD IT?
MAYBE SOMEONE IN THE VILLAGE SAW THEM?
LET'S FIND OUT.
WE CAN'T GO IN THERE LOOKING LIKE THIS.
WHY?
THEY'RE UNDER ATTACK-- PRETTY SURE THEY'RE NOT GONNA BE FRIENDLY TO OUTSIDERS.
HEY--
HOLD STILL-- YOU WANT US TO FIT IN, WE'RE GONNA FIT IN.
COSPLAY FTW!
CAN WE HAVE SIGILS?
RAF...
DON'T SIGIL-BLOCK ME, BRO.

PLAY IT COOL, DUDE.
THIS IS SO AWESOME!
UM, PARDON ME, SIR, MY NAME IS, UH, CINDY OF THE MOON CLAN, WE ARE TRAVELERS FROM--
I DON'T CARE WHO YOU ARE--GRAB A SWORD AND GET TO THE BATTLE!
YOU KNOW HOW TO WORK THAT?
ALL-GIRLS SCHOOL, PLUS ARCHERY, EQUALS--
YOU SOMEHOW JUST GOT HOTTER.
NOBODY'S STOPPING. I KEEP HEARING SOMETHING ABOUT AN ASH KING, WANTS TO BURN THE PLACE TO THE GROUND OR SOME SUCH?
MAYBE WE CAN--
UM, CIN? WE GOT BIGGER FISH.

ROAR!
UM... IS THIS ABOUT THE EGGS WE FOUND? BECAUSE WE LEFT THEM AS-IS! I WOULD NEVER--WE WOULD NEVER--
IS IT SNIFFING US?
IT'S NOT BREATHING FIRE, SO I'M CALLING WHATEVER IT'S DOING A WIN.
SNIFF
PLEASE DON'T KILL US, SMAUG.
MY NAME IS NOT SMAUG.

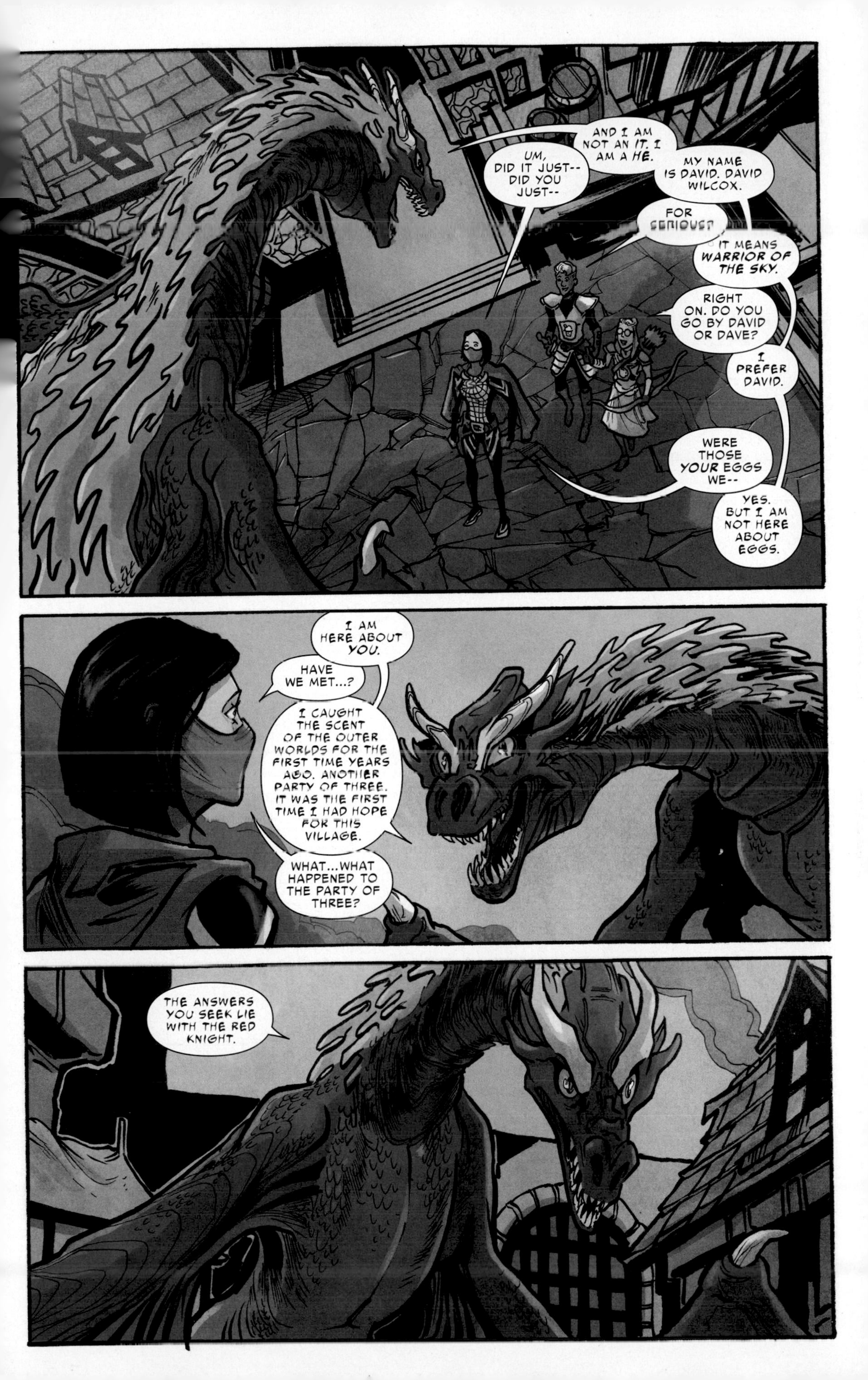
UM, DID IT JUST-- DID YOU JUST--
AND I AM NOT AN IT. I AM A HE.
MY NAME IS DAVID. DAVID WILCOX.
FOR SERIOUS?
IT MEANS WARRIOR OF THE SKY.
RIGHT ON. DO YOU GO BY DAVID OR DAVE?
I PREFER DAVID.
WERE THOSE YOUR EGGS WE--
YES. BUT I AM NOT HERE ABOUT EGGS.
I AM HERE ABOUT YOU.
HAVE WE MET...?
I CAUGHT THE SCENT OF THE OUTER WORLDS FOR THE FIRST TIME YEARS AGO. ANOTHER PARTY OF THREE. IT WAS THE FIRST TIME I HAD HOPE FOR THIS VILLAGE.
WHAT...WHAT HAPPENED TO THE PARTY OF THREE?
THE ANSWERS YOU SEEK LIE WITH THE RED KNIGHT.

RED KNIGHT. AWESOME.
TEAM RED KNIGHT!
SO, WHERE IS THIS RED KNIGHT?
IN THE HEART OF THE BATTLE.
ABOUT TO DIE AT THE HANDS OF THE ASH KING'S ARMY.
BUT YOU APPEARING HERE TODAY, DURING THIS BATTLE...
PERHAPS WE CAN FINALLY TURN THE TIDE.
I HAVE A PLAN. IT WILL MOST LIKELY END IN OUR DEATHS.
YOU HAVE A PLAN? BECAUSE I HAVEN'T SEEN LORD OF THE RINGS IN MONTHS.
I NEED TO TALK TO THE RED KNIGHT. I NEED ANSWERS. SO, LET'S DO YOUR PLAN EXCEPT THE ENDING, 'KAY?

KEEP YOUR SHIELDS UP!
KEEP PRESSING--
--KEEP FIGHTING!
THE TIME HAS COME FOR YOU TO BURN, RED KNIGHT!
RAAARGHH!!!
WHA--
YOU ASKED FOR IT, PAL.

I AM THE MOTHER OF DRAGONS!
WHO?
WE REALLY GOTTA GET YOU HBOGO.
RALLY TO ME, KNIGHTS OF GHEVA!
THE RED KNIGHT'S SURROUNDED-- KEEP CIRCLING!

THWIP
OKAY, RED KNIGHT...
...TAKE YOUR SHOT!
I SHALL, OUTLANDER!
HAVE AT THEE!
NYARGH!
GREAT MOVES, DAVID!
NEXT TIME, WE NEED A SADDLE. I DON'T KNOW HOW KHALEESI DOES IT--
UH, HEY THERE, YOUR KNIGHTLINESS?
MY NAME IS CINDY MOON.

THESE ARE MY FRIENDS. LOLA...
WE'RE GETTING MARRIED.
AND RAFFERTY.
I JUST RODE A TALKING DRAGON.
WE'RE NOT FROM AROUND HERE, BUT...
THESE THREE... THEY ARE TRAVELERS FROM THE OUTER WORLDS.
I COME IN PEACE. PROMISE.
CINDY...?

MOM?!

13

"NARI MOON HAS BEEN MANY THINGS.
"A DOCTOR.
DR. MOON
WEDDING DA
"A PARTNER.
"A MOTHER.
"WHEN I WAS A KID, I BELIEVED MY MOTHER COULD DO *ANYTHING*.
"I *STILL* BELIEVE THAT.
"BUT I NEVER THOUGHT I'D SEE HER AS A *LITERAL* KNIGHT IN SHINING ARMOR."

"HOW DID IT FEEL TO SEE HER AGAIN, CINDY?"

"OVERWHELMING

"AND IT WASN THE BEST PLAC TO CATCH U

"I *DID* MANAGE TO TELL HE HOW I GOT OUT OF THE BUNKER, AND THAT IT WAS *OKAY* FOR ME TO BE OUT. SHE WAS SURPRISED AND BEYOND RELIEVED TO HEAR THE *INHERITORS* WEREN'T A THREAT ANYMORE."

THERE'S TOO MANY OF THEM!

"SHE CRIED.

"THERE WAS A HUG.

"BUT MOSTLY... THERE WAS A LOT OF COMBAT."

AIM FOR THEIR MIDSECTION AND *KEEP PUSHING!* YOUR FATHER IS IN THAT CASTLE, WE HAVE TO RESCUE HIM!

HOW DID DAD GET CAPTURED?

HE WENT LOOKING FOR SOMETHING. GOT CAUGHT INSTEAD.

HOW LONG HAS HE BEEN TRAPPED IN THERE?

IF I WASN'T SO AFRAID HE WAS DEAD, I'D HAVE TO *KILL* HIM FOR BEING SO *STUPID*.

WHAT IF HE'S--
TOO LONG.
JUST KEEP FIGHTING! YOUR FATHER'S ALIVE.
HE HAS TO BE.

"ALBERT MOON SR. HAS BEEN A LOT OF THINGS, TOO.
"A COACH.
COACH MOON
USA
"A TEACHER.
"A FATHER.
"MY DAD HAD TO BE ALIVE. HE HAD TO BE."
YOUR DAYS ARE OVER, RED KNIGHT.
ALL OF THIS DOMAIN SHALL BURN IN THE RIGHTEOUS FIRE OF--
YOUR FACE IS BURNT.
STRONG QUIP, MOM.

ONE MORE PASS! WE'RE ALMOST--
I'M PULLING BACK, THEIR ARCHERS ARE--
RAAARRGHH!
CINDY!
DAMMIT, SHE'S TOO FAR AWAY. I GOT YOU, SWEETHEART, I GOT YOU.
MY LEG...IT'S BROKEN...
C'MON, DAVID. WORK WITH ME HERE, BIG GUY.
CRASH

YOU ARE FINISHED, RED KNIGHT.
PRAY TO YOUR GODS, FOR YOU SHALL SOON MEET THEM.
MOM!
BUT NOT BEFORE WATCHING YOUR DAUGHTER BURN.
"MY FAMILY... WE'VE BEEN THROUGH A LOT.
"BUT THE THING IS...

"WE ALWAYS STUCK TOGETHER..."
WE GOT YOU, KIDDO.
"NO MATTER WHAT."
SHE'S A GOOD TEACHER.
JUST LIKE HER OLD MAN.
HEY, WHO YOU CALLING OLD?
"EVEN WHEN WE COULDN'T BE."
HEY, IT'S ME. YOUR DAD. I...I MADE THESE RECORDINGS FOR YOU SO YOU'D NEVER FEEL--
"WHEN WE'RE TOGETHER...

"THERE'S...
"...NOTHING...
"...WE...
"...CAN'T...
"...DO!"
NOOOOO...!

ARE YOU GUYS--
BROKE MY LEG--I'M GONNA HAVE A CAST!
PRETTY SURE SHE'S CONCUSSED, TOO.
I'M GONNA HAVE A CAST!
SO, THE ASH KING WAS CONNECTED TO ALL THE KNIGHTS, HUH? SWEET.
WE'RE OKAY, CIN. GO FIND YOUR DAD!
SO, BACK HOME, YOU'RE A--
SUPER HERO. YEAH.
WHAT DO THEY CALL YOU?
SILK.
I LIKE IT.

SO, WHAT WAS DAD LOOKING FOR IN THIS DUMP?
OUR FRIEND DR. KAPOOR TRACKED A BLUE SUBSTANCE WITH STRANGE PROPERTIES TO THE NEGATIVE ZONE. WE BELIEVED IT COULD BE SYNTHESIZED INTO AN ANTIDOTE TO WHAT CHANGED YOU.
IT'S A CURE?
IF YOU WEREN'T A SPIDER-PERSON, THEN THE INHERITORS WOULD LEAVE YOU BE, RIGHT? AND YOU COULD GET OUT OF THAT DAMN BUNKER ONCE AND FOR ALL.
WHERE IS DR. KAPOOR?
HE... HE DIDN'T MAKE IT.
I'M...I'M SORRY...
THAT'S NOT ON YOU. THAT'S ON ME.
THIS WHOLE THING IS ON ME.
NOTHING ABOUT YOU NEEDED CURING.
YOU HEAR THAT?
STAY BEHIND ME.
HEY, I'M STILL YOUR MOTHER, SUPER HERO.
...HI THERE, KIDDO...

...MISSED YOU GUYS...
"HE STARTED TO TELL US ABOUT HOW SORRY HE WAS...
DAYS SPENT IN ASH
"HOW HE WAS WRONG, AND THERE WAS NOTHING IN THE CASTLE WORTH FINDING, AND THAT HE FELT BAD PUTTING US ALL AT RISK...
"BUT I WAS TOO BUSY CRYING TO SAY ANYTHING OTHER THAN-- "
MUST GO HOME
DAD.

WHAT WILL WE DO WITHOUT THE RED KNIGHT?
WHAT YOU'VE *ALWAYS* DONE. *FIGHT.*
I--WE--JUST...GAVE YOU A PUSH.
I AM SORRY WE COULD NOT AID YOU IN YOUR SEARCH FOR THE ELIXIR.
IT'S OKAY...
...I HAVE EVERYTHING I NEED NOW.
I WILL WRITE SONGS OF YOUR BRAVERY.
YOU BETTER.
WHERE DID YOUR FATHER WANDER OFF TO?
SORRY, I'M STILL GETTING MY SEA LEGS BACK.
SO...
...SHALL WE GO HOME?

WHEN WE WALKED THROUGH THE PORTAL...IT CLOSED BEHIND US.
WE TRIED TO REOPEN IT FROM THE OTHER SIDE, BUT COULDN'T. WE WERE STUCK IN THE NEGATIVE ZONE. BUT YOU FOUND US.
THANK YOU. ALL OF YOU.
YOU SAID THE PORTAL WAS CLOSED. BUT IT WAS FUNCTIONING NORMALLY WHEN WE GOT HERE. SO...
...WHO REACTIVATED IT?
STORY FOR ANOTHER DAY, I THINK.
TODAY... TODAY I'D LIKE TO SEE MY SON.
RIGHT. OF COURSE, BUT...
...THERE'S SOME STUFF YOU NEED TO KNOW ABOUT ALBERT.
"I TOLD THEM AS GENTLY AS I COULD...

"...ABOUT WHAT HAPPENED TO ALBERT.
"HIS INJURIES. HIS RECOVERIES.
"BUT ALL THAT MATTERED...
HOSPITAL
"...WAS THAT WE WERE ALL TOGETHER. IN ONE ROOM. FINALLY.
SILK HERO of AGES
WHAT A MARVEL
NEW HERO
SILK
LADIES ARE TAKING OVER!
SILK - SPIDER-WOMAN MS. MARVEL, OH MY!
"BUT...I KNOW MY MOM BLAMES HERSELF FOR WHAT HAPPENED TO HIM, TOO."
SILK: HERO OR VILLAIN
YOU GUYS ARE WELCOME TO STAY HERE, Y'KNOW.
WHAT A MARVEL SILK
SILK
MARVEL
ACTUALLY, I GOT A LEAD ON A PLACE FOR US.
ALL OF US.

THERE'S A BIDET IN EVERY BATHROOOM!

WHAT EVEN IS THIS PLACE?
UM, I DON'T WANT TO SOUND UNGRATEFUL, BUT--
CINDY, HOW CAN YOU AFFORD THIS?
IS THIS FROM WHEN YOU WERE A BAD GUY?
YOU WERE A BAD GUY?
NO. KIND OF. I WAS UNDERCOVER.
AND YOU'RE RIGHT. I CAN'T AFFORD THIS.
BUT THE GOOD NEWS IS...

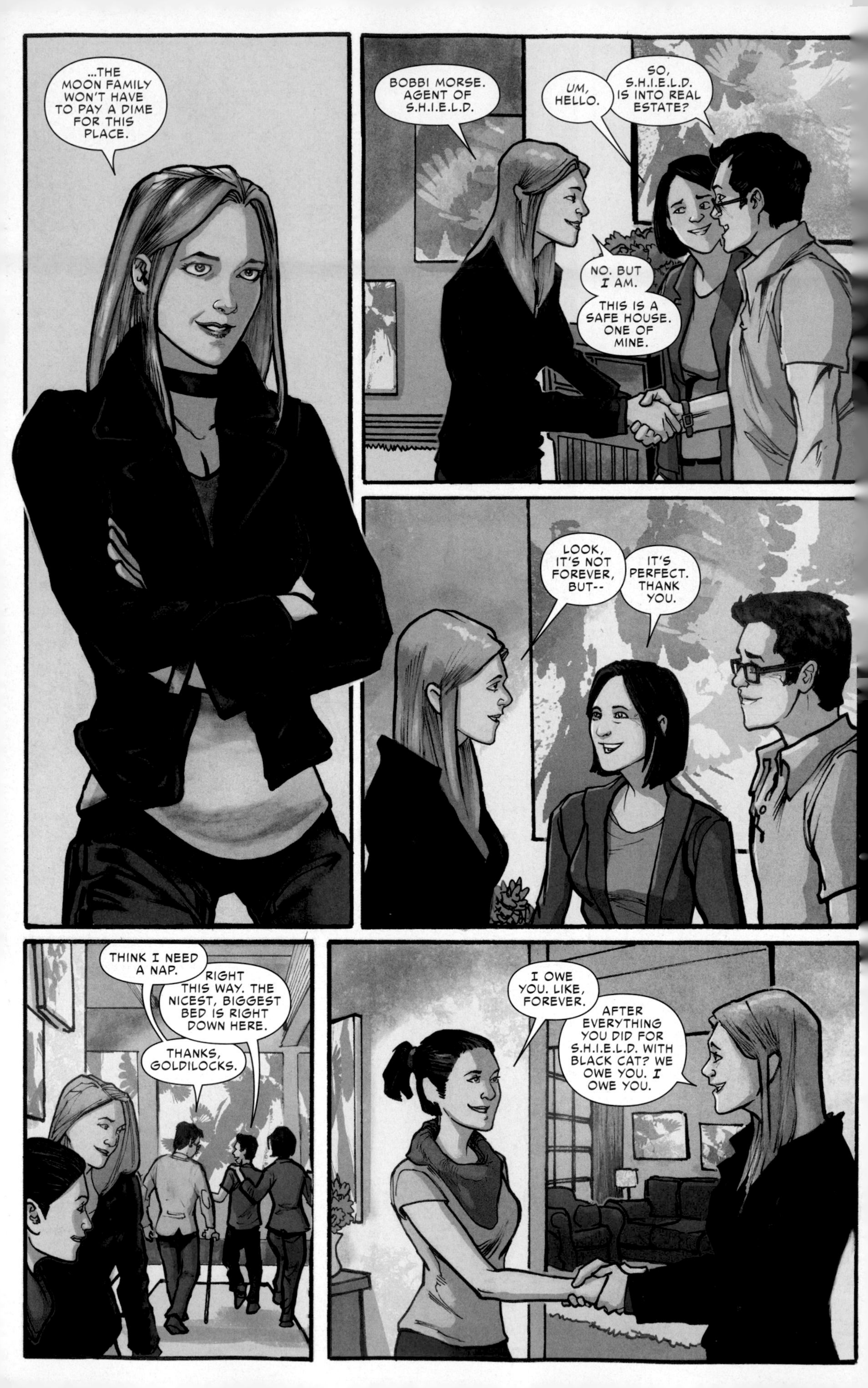
...THE MOON FAMILY WON'T HAVE TO PAY A DIME FOR THIS PLACE.
BOBBI MORSE. AGENT OF S.H.I.E.L.D.
UM, HELLO.
SO, S.H.I.E.L.D. IS INTO REAL ESTATE?
NO. BUT I AM.
THIS IS A SAFE HOUSE. ONE OF MINE.
LOOK, IT'S NOT FOREVER, BUT--
IT'S PERFECT. THANK YOU.
THINK I NEED A NAP.
RIGHT THIS WAY. THE NICEST, BIGGEST BED IS RIGHT DOWN HERE.
THANKS, GOLDILOCKS.
I OWE YOU. LIKE, FOREVER.
AFTER EVERYTHING YOU DID FOR S.H.I.E.L.D. WITH BLACK CAT? WE OWE YOU. I OWE YOU.

...YOU OKAY?
FOR ONCE? I THINK SO.
SO, WHAT'S NEXT?
WHAT DO YOU MEAN?
YOU'VE BEEN LOOKING FOR YOUR FAMILY FOR SO LONG, TOOK THAT JOB AT THE FACT CHANNEL, AND THEN WORKED UNDERCOVER WITH US--NOW YOU HAVE THEM BACK.
SO, I'M WONDERING.
WHAT'S NEXT?
WELL, YOU'VE GOT TIME TO FIGURE OUT WHAT'S NEXT FOR YOU, TOO. AND HEY--
THE OFFER TO SIGN UP WITH S.H.I.E.L.D. STILL STANDS, YOUNG LADY.

"I SLEPT SO WELL THAT FIRST NIGHT. FINALLY FELT LIKE I WAS **HOME.**"
YOU'RE UP EARLY.
IS THAT ANOTHER **NEW** THING ABOUT YOU? YOU'RE AN EARLY RISER AT LAST?
I GUESS SO. YEAH.
WHERE WAS THAT WHEN YOU WERE A TEENAGER?
DAD OKAY?
HE SLEPT WELL. HE'S OUT FOR A WALK NOW.
A WALK? **WHERE?** SHOULD WE--
HE WAS LOCKED UP FOR MONTHS. WANTED TO STRETCH HIS LEGS.
YEAH... I GET THAT.
YOU DON'T HAVE TO WORRY ABOUT ME BEING A SUPER HERO, MOM.
CINDY, I'M YOUR MOM.
I'M **ALWAYS** GOING TO WORRY ABOUT YOU.
I'M JUST GLAD I GET TO DO IT IN PERSON NOW.
"SO, YEAH...
"...IT WAS A WEIRD WEEK..."

...BUT ALSO AN *AMAZING* WEEK.

I'M HAPPY FOR YOU, CINDY.
TRULY.
THANKS, DR. SINCLAIR.

SO...
WHAT *IS* NEXT FOR YOU?

I THINK...I THINK IT'S TIME TO FIGURE OUT WHAT *NORMAL* LOOKS LIKE.
IT FEELS LIKE I'M DUE FOR SOME NORMAL.
*OVER*DUE, I'D SAY.

MIDTOWN.
BIOMETRIC SCAN COMPLETE.
WAITING FOR AUTHORIZATION.
WHERE DID YOUR FATHER WANDER OFF TO?
YOU HAVE A VISITOR FROM THE NEGATIVE ZONE, FANG.
AT LAST. DOES HE HAVE THE PACKAGE?
YES, MA'AM.
PERFECT.
NOW... LET'S PUT AN END TO SILK ONCE AND FOR ALL...
TO BE CONTINUED!